T0082936

DR. JACKSON SPEAKS

HANNAH

(Shut Up Peninnah 'Cause I'm Giving Birth)

"I AM" Fellowship Ministries

Dr. Cecilia Jackson

authorHOUSE®

AuthorHouse™
1663 Liberty Drive
Bloomington, IN 47403
www.authorhouse.com
Phone: 1 (800) 839-8640

Scripture taken from The Holy Bible, King James Version. Public Domain

Published by AuthorHouse 10/03/2017

ISBN: 978-1-5462-1170-9 (sc)
ISBN: 978-1-5462-1169-3 (e)

PREFACE

Hannah is a book that teaches the importance and authority of believers to defeat the voice of the accuser when he comes to rob them of dreams, goals, desires, and the hope of a lively future by stamping "barren" on their spiritual womb. The author's revelations, instructions, spiritual counsel and applicable solutions are both fresh and powerful as revealed through the narrative of Hannah and her encounters with Peninnah! The readers of the book receive fresh understanding and courage to overpower what seems impossible in their own challenges in life including: female rivalry, jealousy, church hurt, emotional pain, unanswered prayers, demonic oppression, male and female relationship quarrels, provision issues, and other difficult areas in daily life. After reading *Hannah*, readers will arise with resolution, bravery, fresh revelation, and a renewed surge of determination that will shift their trials to triumphs.

DEDICATION

To Jewel, my only daughter, whom I saw before you were born. May you always remember that there are no barren places where one allows the waters of God to flow. The Lord's anointing is upon you for good. I love you forever and for always.

To my nieces: Almiria, Adrienne, Ysabelle, Pauleen, Melody, Shelby, Kenya, Jordan, Joy, Hope, Erin, Tracy, Tyauna and Kayla. Know that your life is secure in the palm of His hands, in His purpose for you.

HANNAH

(Shut Up Peninnah 'Cause I'm Giving Birth)

CONTENTS

INTRODUCTION

Hannah

Barren women who became fruitful mothers have historically been the gateway for God's birthing of great kings and mighty men of God. This is true for Samuel who became a great judge and prophet of Israel. His story is one that touches the hearts and emotions of scripture readers like no other. Perhaps because its foundation is in the story of Hannah, one of the Bible's ordinary barren women, the story of Samuel finds its way into the hearts of believers from generation to generation.

The story of Hannah, the mother of Samuel, is found in 1 Samuel and takes place during one of the key turning points of Israel's history. A God-sent man was needed to lead Israel out of the chaotic era of the judges into the flourishing era of the kings. Hannah would give birth to Samuel, who would have a long, significantly influential ministry to Israel. But, it would be through a life of pain, sorrow, rejection and humiliation that the blessing would come.

We want to tell you that you may be going through some pain, suffering, and sometimes humiliation; but your blessing is being prepared for you. And we pray that the blessing you are asking God for will be one that will bless spiritual Israel, the Church today, the kingdom of God, and foremost those lost and dying that Christ came to save.

Hannah's husband Elkanah was from a place called Ramathaim Zophim, which was in the mountains of Ephraim. Ramah was an abbreviated name for Ramathain Zophim, where Samuel was born, worked, lived, died and was buried.

CHAPTER 1

Hannah - Barrenness

God meant for each man to have only one wife and each woman to have one husband (Genesis 2:18, Matthew 19:4-6, 1 Corinthians 7:12). But since His people fell into sin and away from His original blueprint in Genesis, His grace and love tolerated men having more than one spouse – for a season.

Therefore, in those days, polygamy was permissible as part of the culture, so Elkanah had two wives: Peninnah and Hannah. Some theologians assert that Elkanah only took a second wife because of Hannah's barrenness.

We will see the confusion that happens in any home or situation, when people choose to deviate from God's plan. The atmosphere in Elkanah's home became almost unbearable. But out of this "mess" came a miracle. This is why we cannot assess a messy matter unless we have the mind and spirit of discernment. Why? Because God is likely making a miracle from the mess. Man sometimes sees with condemning eyes, so we'll sometimes curse instead of bless others. We'll take our hands off the mess, instead of being an agent of assistance for God to make it a miracle by using our hands. God took Hannah's mess, her barrenness, and made of it a miracle. He will do the same for you.

The wife Peninnah had children, but the wife Hannah was unable to bear children. A common Biblical term used was "barren". Today we use the word infertile, childless, or sterile. When we study the word "barren" very carefully, we will understand the depth of God's message to us today. There are several Hebrew and Greek words associated with barrenness.

- Tsiyah: Literally a parched or **desert land that is under drought, wilderness.** (Jeremiah 51:43, Ezekiel 19:13, Psalms 63:1, Isaiah 41:18) *We have all been in a parched wilderness, feeling like it's a drought and we needed water. Life in the middle of our drought-like situations, our barrenness required water from the Lord's streams of life.*

- Aqar: One with **non-functioning generative organs, whether male or female.** (Genesis 11:30, Exodus 23:26, Deuteronomy 7:14, Judges 13:2-3) *We have sometimes felt – whether man or woman – that we just couldn't produce. Life sometimes just wouldn't come from even our greatest efforts, although we had given all that we had to give, to produce life. We have at some point in life, felt like a non-functioning person.*

- Melechah: **A salted land, dead to life, unable to seed and produce.** (Job 39:6, Psalms 107:34, Jeremiah 17:6) *At times we all have found ourselves in a salty place where it seemed we were just dead and couldn't give life. We felt we couldn't produce even just one seed of life to produce the child we desired. We were in a salty land. What is your baby that you can't seem to push out of your womb alive? Is it still full of life or being chided to death by salt in the mouth of a dream killer? This is your season to come forth and produce.*

- Shakol: To miscarry, to suffer abortion, **literally or figuratively being robbed of a child,** to be empty, to fail to bear fruit, **to cast fruit before the time.** (Genesis 27:45, Exodus 23:26, Leviticus 26:22, Deuteronomy 32:25) *Notice the meaning is loss of life, being robbed of a child – literally or FIGURATIVELY. We lose the true meaning when we don't hear all God is saying. What is the child you seem to be robbed of? What has your enemy come to abort, snatch, or rob from your womb? Getting your GED? Finishing you college degree? Staying clean from drugs a few months longer? Peace in your home? A real marriage relationship with your husband? Or learning to be content until he sends you a husband (or wife)? Your finances? That job that you need so desperately? Just a decent vehicle to drive? Your own home because you're tired of your apartment? You've got a* *book inside you but you still haven't published it? You have ministry you were created to do, yet haven't begun to walk in it? What babies have you miscarried or allowed the enemy to abort? Did you start an endeavor before the season of the Lord, so it seemed not to work and you are now too fearful to get up and go forward, but you're allowing your enemies to about it? It's your season to protect what is in your spiritual womb (you dreams and desires) and give birth.*

- Otser: To **restrain, be enclosed, to hold back and constrain as in close up or detain, to shut up.** (Psalms 107:39, Proverbs 30:16, Isaiah 53:8) *What is keeping you from producing? In this instance you are the one holding back the birth. Why don't you just move forward? Resist the fear and relieve yourself from the burden of not being productive? It's your season of release from the constraints that have held you, detained you and shut off your birthing flow.*

- Argos: An adjective meaning **inactive, unemployed, useless, idle, slow, barren.** (Matthew 12:36, 1 Timothy 5:13, Titus 1:12, James 2:20, 2 Peter 1:8)

Almost every person knows what it means to be shattered and torn, broken to the point that it seems the security of your entire world has fallen apart or is being blown apart. There have been times when many have gone through situations wherein they've felt the tears would never stop, or it would not be a day when they would want to leave a room or a house. Emptiness and void is not uncommon. Many believers have gone through times of emptiness and void (barrenness), when there seemed to be no comfort or no healing agent to help.

During those times you may have felt unproductive, or that you are producing only in small quantities, and there remains areas where you are not fertile, but instead you are dull, arid, uncultivable, parched, uncreative, even blocked.

You may ask, "Is there any formula for moving forward from barrenness to blessedness"? Yes! Absolutely yes!! God has keys that unlock every door that satan (or your own human error) has closed in your life. One of the master keys lies in the life of the story of Hannah – the barren one who gave birth!

CHAPTER 2

Shiloh - A Painful Journey

Among some cultures, barrenness was a family's greatest curse and a woman's greatest shame. It was the ultimate tragedy, because every man's dearest hopes and dreams were to have a child and especially a male child as an heir to continue his name and to inherit his land and possessions.

So Hannah had her **personal sorrow,** but it was an even heavier weight because she could **not fulfill her husband's greatest desire,** to have a child. Compounding Hannah's burdens was **Peninnah**, the fruitful wife of Elkanah, and the issue of going to **Shiloh**.

These are two challenges for you to survive your journey from barrenness to blessedness: silence Peninnah and go to Shiloh!

Elkanah was a direct descendant of Zuph, which would identify his future son, Samuel, as a member of the Kohathite branch of the tribe of Levi and a descendant of Tabernacle and Temple musicians (1 Chronicles 6:16, 22, 26-27, 31–38). Thus, Hannah's husband was a man acquainted with ministry and the responsibilities of such inheritance. Every year he went to Shiloh, which was about sixteen miles from home. The purpose was to worship, celebrate and make sacrifices to God for his blessings upon their home.

1 Samuel 1:1-3 Now there was a certain man of Ramathaimzophim, of mount Ephraim, and his name *was* Elkanah, the son of Jeroham, the son of Elihu, the son of Tohu, the son of Zuph, an Ephrathite: And he had two wives; the name of the one *was* Hannah, and the name of the other Peninnah: and Peninnah had children, but Hannah had no children. And this man went up out of his city yearly to worship and to sacrifice unto the LORD of hosts in Shiloh. And the two sons of Eli, Hophni and Phinehas, the priests of the LORD, *were* there.

These visitations were the festivals and celebrations of the Lord at Shiloh that were commanded by God for Israel to observe as holy and precious meeting times with Him as their God. These were times of worship and rejoicing because of the goodness of their God.

In our day, there are times of coming together to give God worship and praise in the house of our God – church. It is the place where we gather to testify of His goodness, to offer thanks, praise, gladness, and rejoicing. In return, we are strengthened to return home and continue to serve Him diligently in the community. Notice they did not live, stay at Shiloh. They were not so busy at Shiloh that they could not have time for family and community. This is sometimes an error churches make today.

Shiloh was a time of the feasts and festivals for most, but for Hannah it was more like a funeral. As was the custom, Elkanah would praise Peninnah for his sons and daughters and gave them gifts. He loved Hannah and did not want to hurt her feelings since he knew how painful it was for her to see rejoicing over Peninnah's children, yet she could have none. So, on the day he presented his sacrifices (at Shiloh) for Peninnah's children, Elkanah also gave Hannah a portion of the harvest offering. He was a thoughtful husband.

1 Samuel 1:4-5 And when the time was that Elkanah offered, he gave to Peninnah his wife, and to all her sons and her daughters, portions: But unto Hannah he gave a worthy portion; for he loved Hannah: but the LORD had shut up her womb.

Celebration is difficult when it seems that you cannot bring forth the desire of your heart. It's difficult when you're in that empty, void place called *shakol* feeling like you've miscarried your dream or allowed someone or something to abort your child, or you are in that wilderness, salty place, empty, and have failed to bear fruit, lost a dream and are hurting; and it seems everyone else at church is celebrating. Others are at Shiloh offering praise, worship and offerings of thanksgiving to The Lord for all the good things he has done for them! While most were celebrating at Shiloh; for Hannah, Shiloh became a place of pain. The Lord had Hannah on a shelf for a specific season, for a specific time. She was required to endure pain for a time, until she would arise in faith and move forward in her true purpose – to birth a prophet who would save a nation.

CHAPTER 3

Shiloh - the Church in History

The Tabernacle of Moses was God's place of dwelling during the entire wilderness wandering of Israel from Mt. Sinai to Shiloh in the promised land of Canaan. During transit from Sinai, it was covered with particular cloths and coverings. For forty years, it was the place where God set up his church in the wilderness – the meeting or gathering place in the land of Canaan under Joshua's leadership.

It was the place where God set his name. It was functioning through the period of the days of Joshua and the generation that outlived him. It was believed to also span through the period of the book of Judges. The Tabernacle of Moses at Shiloh was where the priests and people of Israel walked through the patterns for church foundation that would be the pillar for understanding Christ and His Church today.

The Word of God states that all the things done in the Old Testament were a shadow, a pattern of things to come (1 Corinthians 10:6, 11). It further states that Jesus himself said the volume of the Book is written about Him, to tell the story and plan for man (Hebrews 10:7 and Psalms 40:6-8).

The first things in scripture are the natural, but they foreshadow the spiritual things to come (1 Corinthians 15:46-47). We are living in the times of the New Testament; therefore we are living in the days of the fulfillment of the Old Testament pattern. The Old was the Law – the external form of truth. Jesus did not come to destroy the Law and the words of the prophets, but to fulfill them (Romans 2:20, Matthew 5:17-18). These are the best of times! Shiloh speaks of the Church and us today, and so does the experience of Hannah!

Even though Biblical worship was fulfilled in the Tabernacle of David and The Temple of Solomon further pictured Christ and patterned the heavenly church and other foundational principals, Moses' Tabernacle from Sinai to Shiloh was the blueprint upon which the progressions of truth rest. See the entire book of Exodus for more in-depth understanding. Also, research Numbers and look for parallels in the New Testament, in Hebrews.

> **Joshua 18:1** And the whole congregation of the children of Israel assembled together at Shiloh, and set up the tabernacle of the congregation there. And the land was subdued before them.

> **Joshua 18:8-10** And the men arose, and went away: and Joshua charged them that went to describe the land, saying, Go and walk through the land, and describe it, and come again to me, that I may here cast lots for you before the LORD in Shiloh. And the men went and passed through the land, and described it by cities into seven parts in a book, and came *again* to Joshua to the host at Shiloh. And Joshua cast lots for them in Shiloh before the LORD: and there Joshua divided the land unto the children of Israel according to their divisions.

> **Joshua 19:51** These *are* the inheritances, which Eleazar the priest, and Joshua the son of Nun, and the heads of the fathers of the tribes of the children of Israel, divided for an inheritance by lot in Shiloh before the LORD, at the door of the tabernacle of the congregation. So they made an end of dividing the country.

> **Joshua 21:2** And they spake unto them at Shiloh in the land of Canaan, saying, The LORD commanded by the hand of Moses to give us cities to dwell in, with the suburbs thereof for our cattle.

(Note: There was a period when Shiloh was the place of the glory of God. This only changed when the Aaronic Priesthood allowed corruption to come into the camp through Eli and his inability to discipline his sons. This prompted the need for God to raise up the prophetic ministry of Samuel from the womb of Hannah. In time, the corrupt condition of Eli's sons precipitated the need for God to raise up and shift to leadership by kings – the first King being Saul.)

CHAPTER 4

Shiloh - the Drama

Let us look more closely into the drama that was taking place at Shiloh. Peninnah and her children were getting positive attention and were the premier pictures of God's blessings, while Hannah was feeling the pain and shame of dreams unfulfilled, miscarried hopes and plans, postponed peace and deferred happiness. She was hurting and empty.

The Bible states that during Hannah's difficult time Peninnah, Hannah's rival, was provoking her severely because of her barrenness and taunting her, laughing at her and scoffing her. Perhaps your Peninnah is saying: you're still in school, you aren't married yet, your church only has 20 members, you're not in your home yet, your kids still aren't saved, I saw your car at Save-A-Lot, you haven't lost that weight yet. The ferocious mean behavior of Peninnah was so severe that it made Hannah cry. Year after year, the same routine would play out and Hannah felt all she could do was just accept the cruel punishment.

Notice that it was during Hannah's weak moments, in her weak area, the area in which she was hurting most, that Peninnah allowed satan to use her to attack Hannah. The woman would attempt to vex Hannah indignantly and annoy her to the point of crass, merciless, humiliation.

Satan will intensify his attack as you come closer to your delivery of your dream, your baby. He will attempt to cause you to miscarry or abort your dream and destiny. He's not omniscient, but he can see external progress and growth just as in the natural you can see the external changes as a woman's belly enlarges during pregnancy. So his threats become sharp and directed to attack and abort the child before delivery, because he can see your external growth. But know that satan does not know the plans for your life. He does not have an inside knowledge or view of what God is doing and desires to do in your life. But, God does and the Father has been onboard, since before you were formed in your mother's womb, to see you through the delivery of your baby, your dreams, alive and well!

The Bible clearly states that Elkanah favored Hannah. So, part of Peninnah's problem was jealously and she used her jealous tongue to enflame Hannah's pain and bring hell's torment (James 3:16) to Hannah's life. Consider that satan is jealous of your position and place in God because he forfeited his. Thus, because of his jealousy, it is satan's tactic to speak things to you that will torment you, like a victim of hell.

> **1 Samuel 1:6-7** And her adversary also provoked her sore, for to make her fret, because the LORD had shut up her womb. And *as* he did so year by year, when she went up to the house of the LORD, so she provoked her; therefore she wept, and did not eat.

The word "adversary" in verse 6, in the Hebrew language (tsaw-raw') is feminine in form and means a female rival who brings affliction, anguish, trouble, and distress.

The word "sore" means, in the Hebrew language, grief, sorrow, wrath, and spite. Furthermore, the word "fret" in verse six means to tumble or become violently agitated, specifically to crash with thunder!

So when we assemble the intent of Peninnah's heart, it means she was a female rival whose purpose was to bring affliction, trouble, and distress, grief, sorrow and anger. It would be so intense that Hannah would be violently agitated enough to thunder and/or be destroyed with thunder. In the same verse understand that the enemy was a female rival, but a few words afterwards the Bible calls the rival a "he". Then the verse reverts to calling the rival a "she". This lets us know that people are used by the devil to provoke believers. Demonic activity is sometimes present and aiming to drive us to a thundering crash.

We can imagine the specific cruel words in English that might have been said to Hannah daily in her life, and said even with more intensity during the time the family was to visit Shiloh!

Do you have an enemy, a rival who is intent on destroying you and bringing you to an ultimate violent crash when you are experiencing pain or hurt, because they thinks they can target you in the areas you are weakest and bring you to a violent end? Hannah loved the Lord, but had to contend with demonic activity. The result was she allowed the Lord to deliver her from her adversary. Furthermore, the Lord kept her whole and safe during the process. This is your pattern. God will deliver you from your adversary and he will keep you whole and safe during the process.

Hannah encountered her Peninnah frequently each day, and especially at the appointed time to worship, praise, and give offerings to the Lord. Note that point carefully. The attacks were timed, calculated, and strategic – directed toward the most opportune times:

> Example: Jesus
> **Luke 4:13** And when the devil had ended all the temptation, he departed from him for a season.

Our Peninnah's, our rivals come:

1) **When we are on the horizon of spiritual breakthrough**. Example: the children of Israel had reached the Jordan and could go no further toward their breakthrough of deliverance without a miracle from God and God silenced their Peninnah with the rod of Moses!

   Exodus 14:13-16 And Moses said unto the people, Fear ye not, stand still, and see the salvation of the LORD, which he will shew to you to day: for the Egyptians whom ye have seen to day, ye shall see them again no more for ever. The LORD shall fight for you, and ye shall hold your peace. And the LORD said unto Moses, Wherefore criest thou unto me? speak unto the children of Israel, that they go forward: But lift thou up thy rod, and stretch out thine hand over the sea, and divide it: and the children of Israel shall go on dry *ground* through the midst of the sea.

2) **When we are experiencing seasons of fruitfulness.** Example: Joseph was esteemed/fruitful before he experienced prison.

   Genesis 49:22-26 Joseph *is* a fruitful bough, *even* a fruitful bough by a well; *whose* branches run over the wall: The archers have sorely grieved him, and shot *at him,* and hated him: But his bow abode in strength, and the arms of his hands were made strong by the hands of the mighty *God* of Jacob; (from thence *is* the shepherd, the stone of Israel:) *Even* by the God of thy father, who shall help thee; and by the Almighty, who shall bless thee with blessings of heaven above, blessings of the deep that lieth under, blessings of the breasts, and of the womb: The blessings of thy father have prevailed above the blessings of my progenitors unto the utmost bound of the everlasting hills: they shall be on the head of Joseph, and on the crown of the head of him that was separate from his brethren.

3) **When we are offering up serious intercession in prayer**. Example: Daniel's intercession for himself and his people precipitated his being put in the den with lions.

Become acquainted with the patterns of impending drama that satan sends in your life; also the drama with regard to Shiloh. Turn the drama into your deliverance. The life of Hannah is a fine example of how this can be done; how one woman changed her barrenness to birthing and birthing a dream that was a personal victory yet simultaneously a birthing that saved a nation.

CHAPTER 5

Weapons - Triumphing over Peninnah

No matter what we face, Jesus has given us a formula and authority to triumph over the strategies of the evil one. One key to ruling over barrenness is wearing the full armor of God.

> **Ephesians 6:10-17** Finally, my brethren, be strong in the Lord, and in the power of his might. Put on the whole armour of God, that ye may be able to stand against the wiles of the devil. For we wrestle not against flesh and blood, but against principalities, against powers, against the rulers of the darkness of this world, against spiritual wickedness in high *places*. Wherefore take unto you the whole armour of God, that ye may be able to withstand in the evil day, and having done all, to stand. Stand therefore, having your **loins girt about with truth**, and having on the **breastplate of righteousness**; And your **feet shod with the preparation of the gospel of peace**; Above all, taking the **shield of faith**, wherewith ye shall be able to quench all the fiery darts of the wicked. And take the **helmet of salvation**, and the **sword of the Spirit, which is the word of God:**

Apply your armor directly to the child you think you have been robbed of! What is Peninnah taunting you about? What is the area that seems to be a wilderness, salty, and won't give life? Use the armor appropriated for you to triumph. If you don't wear it, you can't win the battle. Instead, your Peninnah will win daily, and with every opportunity drive you mercilessly to a thundering end. Tell Peninnah to "shut up" because you're giving birth! You are going to see life and victory in your situation.

It doesn't matter if it's:
- Getting your GED
- Finishing your college degree
- Staying clean from drugs a few months longer
- Obtaining peace in your home
- Developing a real marriage relationship with your husband
- Or learning to be content until God sends you a husband
- An increase in your finances
- That job that you need so desperately
- Just a decent vehicle to drive
- Your own home because you're tired of your apartment
- A book, a journal, a ministry, a business you're pregnant with

What babies have you miscarried or allowed the enemy to abort? Did you start your project before the timing of the Lord, so it seemed not to work and you are too fearful to get up and go forward! We challenge you to use the key of your armor of God and unlock every door the enemy, or your own human errors have closed.

> **Ephesians 6:14-17** Stand therefore, having your **loins girt about with truth**, and having on the **breastplate of righteousness**; And your **feet shod with the preparation of the gospel of peace**; Above all, taking the **shield of faith**, wherewith ye shall be able to quench all the fiery darts of the wicked. And take the **helmet of salvation**, and the **sword of the Spirit, which is the word of God:**

Verse 6:14 says **speak the truth of what scripture says about you;** what God's promises to you are and walk in truth as a lifestyle. Righteousness is not a culture of the past for ancient Bible believers and old time saints. It is the way of the Lord if you want dreams to come true.

Verse 6:15 says **walk in peace according to the Bible's definition of peace.** Avoid being out of control and dwelling with others who have not mastered the control of their own human spirit. Be one who will settle any argument when you are present, with a word of peace from the gospel. Let this armor function at home, at work, at leisure, at church, wherever you are. Furthermore, **let the gospel of peace keep your own heart** when temptations come to make you fearful and unsteady. Remember that the Lord holds the helm to the ship of your life.

Verse 6:16 encourages us to **use faith as our shield to repel any darts of fire that the evil one directs our way**, and to believe what God said and what He put in your heart. Your faith will form a shield to protect your vision, your dream, the desire God placed in your heart. Your faith is an offensive tool to walk you forward to and through anything.

Verse 6:17 says you must **know Jesus as Savior, Lord, and King**. Your sure foundation in salvation gives you what you need to win nations for Christ, to go into the streets and highways and compel men to know Christ through the witness of your life and the words of life that will come from you. Furthermore, the Word of God is a sword that is sharp on both sides to call things that are not into existence and to cut down and destroy those doctrines and words that are not of Christ and are sent to destroy any plan he has set into motion in your spiritual womb. **Learn the Word of God. Live by it. Use it to create life**.

There is absolutely no need to fear any degree of drama. Just deal with it using the weapons God has given you. Our weapons are mighty and destroy strongholds of imagination and thoughts that may come as a result of the wicked one. He lurks trying to invade our thought realm with strong disbelief and attempts to re-direct us away from the Father and from our God given purpose. The negative efforts will fall useless and lifeless in the light of the Word of God.

> **Isaiah 52:7** How beautiful upon the mountains are the feet of him that bringeth good tidings, that publisheth peace; that bringeth good tidings of good, that publisheth salvation; that saith unto Zion, Thy God reigneth!

> **Romans 10:15** And how shall they preach, except they be sent? As it is written, how beautiful are the feet of them that preach the gospel of peace, and bring glad tidings of good things!

CHAPTER 6

Shiloh - Let Us Go Into the House of The Lord

In 1 Samuel 1:7, we read that year-by-year, when Hannah went to the house of the Lord, she was so provoked she wept and would not eat. Her responses to Peninnah's attacks were so severe that her appetite for natural food was taken. She did not eat for long periods of time; therefore her husband Elkanah became concerned and approached her about it.

> **1 Samuel 1:6-8** And her adversary also provoked her sore, for to make her fret, because the LORD had shut up her womb. And *as* he did so year by year, when she went up to the house of the LORD, so she provoked her; therefore she wept, and did not eat. Then said Elkanah her husband to her, Hannah, why weepest thou? And why eatest thou not? And why is thy heart grieved? *Am* not I better to thee than ten sons?

Note that attacks on Hannah came around the visits to Shiloh, the house of the Lord. This is an interesting timing of the enemy. Satan tries to humiliate us, bring affliction and anguish, trouble, and distress us when we are going to unify with other believers. He attempts to cause grief, sorrow, wrath, and spite, and to tumble or cause us to become violently agitated at a time when we should be rejoicing in anticipation of enjoying God's presence and celebrating in the house of the Lord. The assault is on our time, our place of prayer, our worship, our time of offering thanksgiving and sacrifices of praise and tithes and offerings to the Lord our God. The special pilgrimage time was a time of delight for Peninnah to intensify what she had been doing daily in Hannah's life.

Be aware and sabotage, incapacitate and disrupt the enemy's desire to stop your visits to Shiloh. Shiloh represents several important truths to every believer, and especially every leader who desires to fulfill God's dream and vision. Our God will always pour in more grace, promises, healing and strength when the Peninnah in your life tries to destroy you. Tell Peninnah to "shut up". You're going to Shiloh and you WILL give birth!

Let your heart be made stronger as you read these words. Don't stay away from the church – rather – run to the church: Shiloh (the gathering house for believers) is:
- The place where barrenness (spiritual, emotional and physical) is turned into fruitfulness, victory, and joy in God
- Is a place of vision in a world that cannot see
- A place of plenty in the midst of famine
- A place to meet God and obtain the otherwise inaccessible desires of the heart
- A place where prophets are birthed, grow, mature, and function in God's grace
- A place from which the Word of the Lord goes forth to all nations
- A place where the people of God gather and give God praise and glory for keeping his promises and caring for their every need
- A place where discernment is keen and justice prevails
- A place where the enemy is blocked in his attempts to twist the vision and his hold on God's people is destroyed
- A place of comfort and peace, hope and victory
- A place where a believer can return to God for His glory the use of gifts he has given to believers
- A place where believers are edified, exhorted, comforted, and lovingly admonished
- A place of refuge and safety and rest in His Presence from harsh storms and winds of life

- A place of Godly counsel
- A place where solid foundations are laid in the lives of believers so they can mature
- A place where the five-fold ministry is guided by God for the perfecting of the saints and the work of ministry

Hebrews 10:25 Not forsaking the assembling of ourselves together, as the manner of some *is;* but exhorting *one another:* and so much the more, as ye see the day approaching.

Refuse the voice of Peninnah who would keep you from your Shiloh. To stay away from Shiloh is to separate and isolate yourself, and to eventually become a law unto yourself, which will lead to a level of pride that will lead to your destruction.

Run to Shiloh! Shiloh is a vital part of God's Kingdom. Do not let mistakes church leaders have made in your past or false representations of the church, dissuade you from believing in the "true" church that scriptures confirm to be the Bride of Christ! The Lord is pulling down and unmasking false churches and is raising up and establishing true Kingdom believers who are being birthed from the presence of God and are being established as true pastors to lead true Kingdom churches. These churches, lead by Godly pastors, will triumph and lead victorious people for the advancement of the Kingdom of God. Shiloh is a valuable part of God's Kingdom and a fruitful place where the Lord desires his people to gather.

CHAPTER 7

Intercession - Prayer and Worship Unharnessed

One day Hannah had enough of being sick and tired of her miserable situation. One evening while the family was in town for the celebrations, after they had eaten supper and had something to drink with the meal, Hannah left the others at the tent and went over to the Tabernacle. Eli the priest was sitting at the customary place close to the entrance.

In the temple that evening, Hannah turned to the Lord, and through intercessory prayer, broke her chains of barrenness. She took her pain, sorrow and grief to God. Although she had bitter experiences, she did not embrace bitterness to the extent that it marred her soul. 1 Samuel 1:11–19 is the recording of Hannah's Song. It is as powerful, anointed, and beautiful as any psalm in the Book of Psalms written by David and other musicians. She started by making a vow:

> **1 Samuel 1:11** And she vowed a vow, and said, O LORD of hosts, if thou wilt indeed look on the affliction of thine handmaid, and remember me, and not forget thine handmaid, but wilt give unto thine handmaid a man child, then I will give him unto the LORD all the days of his life, and there shall no razor come upon his head.

The Israelites were already trained that whatever were the first fruits of a harvest belonged to God anyway, even the first born of the flock. So it was not difficult for Hannah to vow to give her son back to Eli the priest as a gift to God when he was born.

She knew Samuel, her son, would be trained by Eli to be of service in the house of God. Samuel was given as a Nazirite. When Hannah was praying in the Temple, only her lips moved. For years she had held in the secret room of her heart, a personal desire, a dream in despair that would eventually birth this powerful prayer. She could only pray honestly and share with God the hurts and pains she had held for years and years on her life's journey. This was her place of hiding where it was just her and God and she could pour out to Him all of her cup, which she could no longer carry alone. It was a prayer of petition passionately and earnestly given to God.

Notice in her prayer, her initial recognition of her "Lord of Hosts"! Hannah expressed her faith in God's vast greatness. It was this positioning of God as the greatest of everything, of multitudes seen and unseen (Lord of Hosts), which automatically placed her as a humble servant asking for a great miracle from a great God!

This is what the Lord is asking of you -- to make fruitful those barren places in areas of your life. Pour your heart out to Him in all honesty, not hiding anything, yet recognizing His vast greatness and omnipotent ability to grant your requests. This woman was so deeply involved in her conversation that the spiritually dull priest thought she was intoxicated. By this time in Israel's history, Eli and his sons had begun to walk in disobedience to God, so his spiritual eyes and ears were dull. Otherwise he would have been able to discern Hannah's state and know that she was not drunk, but was in travail and in deep prayer.

Nevertheless, her intoxication with God's presence shows that she was in a place in God's presence in prayer where it did not matter how man assessed her. It was right there in prayer that she won the triumphant victory over barrenness. It was right in that place of prayer that she became a fruitful womb by the miracle touching hand of God. Hannah was conceiving her child Samuel, by faith, right there in God's overwhelming presence while praying!! This is where the birthing begins. You cannot birth anything you have not labored for in the natural. It is the same in the spiritual realm. You cannot birth a manifestation of dreams and goals unless you have labored and travailed in prayer for them.

How will you give birth to that dream, that child you are carrying? When will you see the manifestation of what's internal become external? When will you see the birthing (manifestation) of the dream(s) you thought you lost, but they are still alive in your womb, saying now it's time to have faith to conceive and birth this vision in your intercession? It's time to conceive in your private prayer with Him, in His presence, the thing(s) that will be manifested/birthed publically. Spend some time with God right there. And before you know it, it will be time to bear down and push out your dream.

Transitioning something from the dream realm to the realm of manifestation by faith takes effort, much like a natural pregnancy. You nurture the child/dream even in its infancy, pre-surface stages. Then when the time comes to push it forth, you release with confidence knowing that it's the right season and all will be well!

When Eli saw her mouth moving, but heard no words, he accused her of being drunk, but Hannah proclaimed to the man of God that she was not a daughter of the devil, but a woman who was sad and hurt and pouring her soul out to the Lord. Hannah spoke to the Lord out of the great grief in her heart, believing God would answer her prayers!

> **1 Samuel 1:12-16** And it came to pass, as she continued praying before the LORD, that Eli marked her mouth. Now Hannah, she spake in her heart; only her lips moved, but her voice was not heard: therefore Eli thought she had been drunken. And Eli said unto her, How long wilt thou be drunken? put away thy wine from thee. And Hannah answered and said, No, my lord, I *am* a woman of a sorrowful spirit: I have drunk neither wine nor strong drink, but have poured out my soul before the LORD. Count not thine

handmaid for a daughter of Belial: for out of the abundance of my complaint and grief have I spoken hitherto.

This prayer was unharnessed and unrestrained by the thoughts of man. From Hannah's mouth, a woman who was totally free and flowing like a fountain of freedom, came an earnest prayer that would reach God without restraint and produce an answer. Some people say you should not go to God complaining and expect an answer; but Hannah said it was out of her abundance of complaint and grief that she spoke to God. And He answered her!

Conceive your Samuel while in intercessory prayer, while travailing. This is where this barren woman gained the faith to conceive Samuel and give birth to him. Hannah actually conceived Samuel in prayer by faith, then she gave birth later to what was in her womb as a result of an encounter with the mighty God! The conceiving actually takes place during your prayer, by faith, while you are with the Lord of Hosts. This being true – the evidence will soon be seen by all.

CHAPTER 8

Go in Peace - Petition Granted

After Hannah responded to Eli, asking him to not consider her a woman of the devil, but to understand that she only moved and acted out of the great burden that she carried, Eli prayed for her that the God of Israel would grant her the request of her heart. This may have been the last true prayer that the fallen priest made, but it was one aligned with God's heart.

> **1 Samuel 1:17-18** Then Eli answered and said, Go in peace: and the God of Israel grant *thee* thy petition that thou hast asked of him. And she said, Let thine handmaid find grace in thy sight. So the woman went her way, and did eat, and her countenance was no more *sad*.

When Hannah left Shiloh that evening, her entire countenance had changed! The spirit of sadness had been lifted. Because she prayed, change was inevitable. She conceived her answer while in travailing prayer with her God. You must pray in faith with a passion pleading from your pain, believing your help has already come. Sometimes, others will not be able to pray with the conviction and passion that you can petition God with. You go into His presence and make your request known. This was a <u>personal</u> experience. Some things you need no support on, just do what is required of you for personal change.

The scriptures read that Elkanah's family got up early the next day and went to church at Shiloh one more time before leaving to return home to Ramah. The next time Elkanah had intercourse with Hannah, because she had conceived by faith in prayer, she naturally conceived during intercourse with her husband! Why? It's because the Lord remembered her request. She had a son in due time and named him Samuel. The name Samuel means, "asked of God". In other words, her prayer aligned in perfect timing with her coming together with Elkanah because she asked of God, and in response she received what she asked him for.

Don't let anyone determine your spirit and attitude when you pray. I have heard Christians say one should not go before God when in pain, hurting, or when frustrated. Hannah is proof that, when in need, we can go to God in any state we find ourselves. A songwriter wrote a song titled "Just As I Am....you bid me come to thee, Lamb of God". To break the barrenness and have the child, you must conceive in intercession, go just as you are. The Lord bids you to come to him. It is part of your benefits of His shed blood and being an heir of salvation. You can ask what you want, and in faith you will receive it.

> **1 Samuel 1:19-20** And they rose up in the morning early, and worshipped before the LORD, and returned, and came to their house to Ramah: and Elkanah knew Hannah his wife; and the LORD remembered her. Wherefore it came to pass, when the time was come about after Hannah had conceived, that she bare a son, and called his name Samuel, *saying,* Because I have asked him of the LORD.

The next visit to the temple, only Peninnah and her children went to the celebration, because Hannah would not go to Shiloh until she had completed her vow to bring Samuel and leave him there with Eli indefinitely. This would be after she had finished breast-feeding the boy. So she stayed home, and they returned when Samuel was weaned.

At that time, Hannah took the child and gifts of sacrifice to Eli the priest and gave Samuel to Eli to train for the work of ministry in the Temple.

Samuel became a prophet, priest and judge in Israel, serving God and His people in righteousness and honor. Hannah's personal desire and commitment to intercessory prayer not only changed her life and her family, but also shifted an entire nation!

When God blesses you and makes you fruitful in areas of your life where you have painfully waited and felt like a failure, take the time to give the Lord gifts of praise, and worship Him for His goodness and faithfulness and His kindness to you.

Then, give your gift back to the Lord by finding a way to use what He has done for you to bless the Lord and further Kingdom ministry, which is the work of the Lord in the lives of people in the world.

Someone needs you to speak into their life about what you have gone through and even what you are going through, as you have conceived and are about to deliver the child of your hopes and dreams. You can teach and encourage others how to silence Peninnah, go to Shiloh and give birth.

You may need to encourage someone because you have stayed free from drugs now for one year, or have finally gotten your home after years of apartment living. Or you may have finally sold your home and can move into a condominium suitable for your present lifestyle. Or perhaps your adult child has come to the Lord after you conceived the change during your intercessory prayer and you now see the results birthed.

Perhaps someone needs to know that you now have your diploma after being told for years you couldn't do it. Or someone else needs to know you now drive your own vehicle after years of cabs and riding the bus.

What or who is your Samuel that you are rejoicing and giving God thanks for after your Hannah experience? Your assignment is also for you to minister to someone else so they too can have a Hannah experience.

> **1 Samuel 1:21-28** And the man Elkanah, and all his house, went up to offer unto the LORD the yearly sacrifice, and his vow. But Hannah went not up; for she said unto her husband, *I will not*

go up until the child be weaned, and *then* I will bring him, that he may appear before he LORD, and there abide for ever. And Elkanah her husband said unto her, Do what seemeth thee good; tarry until thou have weaned him; only the LORD establish his word. So the woman abode, and gave her son suck until she weaned him. And when she had weaned him, she took him up with her, with three bullocks, and one ephah of flour, and a bottle of wine, and brought him unto the house of the LORD in Shiloh: and the child *was* young. And they slew a bullock, and brought the child to Eli. And she said, Oh my lord, *as* thy soul liveth, my lord, I *am* the woman that stood by thee here, praying unto the LORD. For this child I prayed; and the LORD hath given me my request which I asked of him: Therefore also I have lent him to the LORD; as long as he liveth he shall be lent to the LORD. And he worshipped the LORD there.

CHAPTER 9

Hannah - Sing Your Song

After Hannah made her vow to the Lord before Eli the priest, she prayed again. This prayer is known as a song of praise to the Lord expressing her gratitude for God delivering her from Peninnah's taunting and granting her the desires of her heart.

This song is recorded in 1 Samuel 1:1-10. It is sometimes called "Hannah's Song" because it is written in the spirit and tone of many of the psalms of David in the Book of Psalms. The words of joy and victory from the depths of Hannah's heart sprang up into a beautiful melody from her to God!

The lyrics are paraphrased as this: My heart rejoices in the Lord and I am now stronger in the Lord. I can smile at my enemies because I am happy in your deliverance and help. There is no one who is holy like the Lord and there is none beside you and there is no rock like our God.

Do not speak proudly or let prideful comments come from your mouth because the Lord is a God of knowledge and by Him the quality of all deeds are measured. The weapons of the mighty men are destroyed and those who are weak are given strength.

Those who are satisfied earn wages for bread and those who are hungry are not hungry any more; so that those who are barren have given birth to seven children and the one who has many children is languished and sick.

The Lord puts to death and makes alive. He lowers one to death and He raises others up. The Lord makes poor and He makes rich; He lowers and lifts up. He raises the poor from dust and lifts the poor beggars and homeless from the heap of a life of rubbish. He places those whom He delivers among the noble causing them to inherit the kingdom of God.

The very foundations of the earth are the Lord's. He will guard the feet of His believers but the wicked will be left alone and quiet in their darkness. Because of strength only, no man shall prevail. The enemies of the Lord shall be broken in pieces and the God of heaven shall thunder his wrath against them.

The Lord will judge even until the ends of the earth and time. He will strengthen His royal people and lift up the power and voice of His anointed.

> **1 Samuel 2:1-10** And Hannah prayed, and said, My heart rejoiceth in the LORD, mine horn is exalted in the LORD: my mouth is enlarged over mine enemies; because I rejoice in thy salvation. *There is* none holy as the LORD: for *there is* none beside thee: neither *is there* any rock like our God. Talk no more so exceeding proudly; let *not* arrogancy come out of your mouth: for the LORD *is* a God of knowledge, and by him actions are weighed. The bows of the mighty men *are* broken, and they that stumbled are girded with strength. *They that were* full have hired out themselves for bread; and *they that were* hungry ceased: so that the barren hath born seven; and she that hath many children is waxed feeble. The LORD killeth, and maketh alive: he bringeth down to the grave, and bringeth up. The LORD maketh poor, and maketh rich: he bringeth low, and lifteth up. He raiseth up the poor out of the dust, *and* lifteth up the beggar from the dunghill, to set *them* among princes, and to make them inherit the throne of glory: for the pillars of the earth *are* the LORD'S, and he hath set the world upon them. He will keep the feet of his saints, and the wicked shall be silent in darkness; for by strength shall no man prevail. The adversaries of the LORD shall be broken to pieces; out of heaven shall he thunder upon them: the LORD shall judge the

ends of the earth; and he shall give strength unto his king, and exalt the horn of his anointed.

Just as the scripture records Hannah's song, you and I have a prayer and a song exalting the Lord for all He has done for us! If you do not have a song, you will have a song as you walk through the valleys of your life and cry out in travailing prayer and intercessory prayer to conceive your miracle!

Tell Peninnah to shut up, 'cause you're giving birth! You are going to Shiloh and you will give back to the Lord of Hosts because of His goodness to you.

CHAPTER 10

Conclusion

There are several mothers in Hebrew history such as Sarah, Rebekah, Leah, Rachael and Elizabeth, who were barren but God intervened. Have no doubt. He will intervene for you!!

Remember, your moment of greatest opportunity can become the opportune time for satan's greatest attack, but your weapons are mightier than any attack launched against you. Know that the Peninnah's in your life will try to keep you from Shiloh, but the resources at Shiloh are what you need to establish and maintain your victory. Shiloh is part of the kingdom plan.

Be aware that your victory is conceived in your time of prayer when you pour out your heart to the Lord – withholding nothing. Know that the more the enemy tries to destroy, greater is the outpouring of God's grace in your life to triumph over satan and reach the goals he thought he robbed from you.

Remember that when you use the weapons God has given you, every imagination and stronghold coming against you will be disarmed and broken.

When you give birth in the areas where you were barren, don't forget to go back to Shiloh, sing your song and give thanks and worship to God for his goodness. Don't forget to use your blessings for the work of the ministry, which is to bless others.

God blessed Hannah with the desires of her heart and made her a fruitful womb. She gave birth to Samuel who later became a prophet and a judge. He lived for a time in Ramah, close to Jerusalem; he built an altar to the Lord and administered justice to all of Israel. It was he who warned the people about the dangers of kingship, however they rejected his admonition. God confirmed the truth of his warning by later allowing Israel to have a king rule over them.

God revealed to Samuel that he would anoint a Benjaminite (Saul) as king of Israel. For a time, Saul depended on Samuel for God's instructions, but later did not hear him, nor hear God. The final plight of this king greatly impacted Israel.

Eventually, Samuel was the prophet who was commissioned to anoint David, the son of Jesse as Israel's king. Hannah's miracle became a blessing to the people of God. He is doing the same for you! Your miracle is not only for you, but somehow it will have the capacity to be a blessing for the people of God, thus impacting the Kingdom. Your *testimony* of deliverance can also bless unbelievers as a part of the planting and watering process of them coming to Christ.

The spiritual rains are falling on the fields in the earth today and there is fresh water for your field. Come and drink freely from heaven's fountain so you will be positioned to be used of God, to receive and to water a coming great harvest of people who do not know Jesus, but need to drink from the life that is in you.

Peninnah gave birth to several children and not too much was mentioned of them in scripture; but Hannah gave birth to one child who was a **prophet**, **priest** and **king** of Israel. **HER BIRTHING CHANGED A NATION!!**

You were birthed to change a nation is some manner and in some area or areas. Your birthing was decided before you existed on this planet. Your birthing and the plan for your life were pre-determined by the Father and Creator of mankind. Creation is groaning for you to manifest this purpose for which you were created, so that you will give birth to the dreams and plans in you that were placed there by the Father even before chronological. In this season of birthing, the Holy Spirit will also cause you to deliver that promise which will change you, your family, community, city and nation.

In Jeremiah 29:11 the scripture says God knows the plans he has for you; plans for your good and not your disaster, plans for a positive and powerful life that you can expect to walk through daily and journey to a productive and successful end.

2 Timothy 1:9 states God has saved us and called us with a holy calling (which means everything a believer is called to do is for his holy purpose: a holy accountant, a holy chemist, a holy evangelist, a holy pilot or bus driver, etc.). This scripture states that we were not called according to our own dictates, but according to God who dictated our **PURPOSE** and the grace of God which was given to us in Christ Jesus **BEFORE THE WORLD BEGAN** (before chronological time began) to secure that we will accomplish our purpose.

This means before chronological time, God had already established your purpose. The Greek word for "purpose" in this scripture is "Prothesis" – meaning the setting forth of a favorable, intentional statement exposed before God as was the bread on the Temple table and as a story written skillfully and expertly. The root word is "thesis", which means a narrative, essay, or composition that follows an expository pattern based on the main statement which is called a "thesis" statement.

How empowering to know the love and power of God who knows the calling [the baby (dream, desire)] we are destined to birth which was given to us according to God's intentional, favorable statement before we were even born. The narrative, essay, composition, writing about our life, our calling was exposed, written and laid out before the very Godhead and the angels as the bread was laid upon the Temple table according to His Grace given to us before the world began!!

This truth should encourage you to take authority over Peninnah's intimidation and GIVE BIRTH to your purpose and dream.

Author's Annotations

Annotation #1: The Era of the Judges

The death of Joshua brought about a new situation in Israel's history and in the lives of the people. They were now independent in their own homeland and for the first time they did not have a strong "single" leader. Moses and Joshua had been the General, the Prime Minister, and the Chief Rabbi and the people had responded to them. This quality of leadership did not come often, so the vacuum of leadership created by the death of Joshua lead to many challenges.

Before Joshua died he conquered about 90% of the Land and divided it among the tribes, then disbanded the great army he had used to fulfill the promise to bring the people into the Promised Land.

The center points of Jewish life began to dissipate:
a) Instead of one Jewish people, there were <u>12 tribes</u> who had loose allegiances with one another
b) There was a lack of central <u>government</u> and central authority
c) There was little <u>religious authority in many ways, although they still had the Tabernacle of Moses</u> (outlining God's order for government and religious order at the time)
d) There was <u>competition for private altars and private interpretation</u> of how and when to sacrifice; eliminating the need to gather corporately and worship
e) An Era of almost <u>continual warfare</u> ensued as there was a <u>continuous infiltration of the enemy</u> who had been driven out of the land

In summary, there was a period when seemingly everyone did what was right in their "own" eyes (Judges 17:5-6).

Even though there were 15 Judges, some of whom did right in the site of the Lord as God always will have those who will stand for him even in the darkest times, problems and conflict still controlled Israel.

This sad state of affairs would continue until the time of Samuel – until the time when one barren woman would not give up on her desire to give birth - until Hannah kept pushing into the presence and into the heart of Father and made a promise that she would give back to the Lord her "baby" when the Lord blessed her. The impact of Hannah's determination was pivotal in Israel's history.

Annotation #2: Medical -health field definitions

Miscarriage

> "natural" death of an embryo or fetus in the womb; it generally takes place in the early stages of prenatal development before the fetus or embryo is able to survive on its own. It is the mother's body removing the fetus on its own; she generally has no choice in the termination of the pregnancy and the act of loss is not deliberate. Many reasons and all are not known: health issues, infection, disease – kidney, thyroid, heart, diabetes exposure to environmental and workplace hazards, hormonal or uterine abnormalities, incompetent cervix (it widens too early, opens too early), lifestyle of smoking and drinking alcohol or use of drugs, immune system disorders, use of medications, emotional and mental stresses, and many unknown reasons.

> **close to ¼ pregnancies end in miscarriage

Abortion

> the ending of a pregnancy by removal or forcing out from the womb of a fetus or embryo before it is able to survive on its own.

It is a deliberate act to keep the embryo from gong full term. Abortion often can be assisted via chemical or surgical induction.

Some socioeconomic challenges include: social pressures, preference for sex of a child, no child wanted due to singlehood, early motherhood, insufficient economic support, and rejection of contraceptives personal preferences, population control, disconnect with father, health issue risks etc.

These medical definitions parallel to what can happen with our dreams and goals. Do not allow anyone to convince you to avoid your baby (spiritually). No matter what the challenge to hold onto their dream; follow Hannah's pattern. Don't allow forced abortion of your dreams, your destiny. Avoid listening to infectious negative words that will cause you to miscarry your baby. Allow nothing or no one to be a hazard to your mental, emotional, physical, or spiritual health. Pray and deliver your baby.

Annotation #3: Power Over Principalities

Elkanah, Hannah's husband was a direct descendant of Zuph, thus Samuel (his future son) would be a member of the Kohathite branch of the tribe of Levi and a descendant of the Tabernacle and Temple musicians (1 Chronicles 6:4, 6, 9, 16, 22, 26-27, 31-38).

Kohathite was a branch of the sons of the Tribe of Levi appointed by David to minister daily before the Ark of the Covenant in David's Tabernacle. They had direct access to the veil (the Presence of God) opposite to Moses's Tabernacle where only the High Priest on the Day of Atonement was the only time the priest could go before God. David's 3 leaders were Asap (a Gershite), Heman (a Kohathite), and Ethan (Jeduthan, a Merarite)

Thus, Hannah's husband was well acquainted with ministry and its responsibilities. Each year he went to Shiloh, which was about 16 miles from home.

Become acquainted with your benefits as a royal New Covenant priest. Study to understand, prayer and worship, the lifestyle of a Kingdom believer. Always find time to study God's Word with qualified teachers who can keep you sure-footed and understanding Kingdom principles.

Annotation #4: Understanding Shiloh

This was a period when Shiloh was the place of the Glory of God. This only changed when Aaron became corrupt when Eli would not discipline his unruly sons.

Shiloh was the inhabitation of God for the children of Israel during the wandering from Mt. Sinai, to Shiloh in the Promised Land. Shiloh was the central meeting place of religious life for the congregation of Israel.

Annotation #5: Peninnah's Core/Jealousy

Do not allow the aggravation launched against your destiny and delivery to cause you to need deliverance from demonic strongholds. If you find yourself in this position, seek a "true – God lead deliverance ministry" and get delivered. Satan's pursuit against you does NOT have to prevent you from achieving your destiny and delivering to the earth domain what God has placed in you. The entirety of creation and the creature is groaning for you to come forth (Romans 8:19).

Jealousy's demonic manifestations include:

Anger	Revenge
Murder	Spite
Cruelty	Rage
Hatred	Envy
Contention	Strife
Extreme Competition	
Cause Divisions	

(Genesis 4:8; 4:4-6; Proverbs 6:34, 10:12, 13:10, 14:16-17, 14:29-30, 22:24-25, 27:4, 29:22-23, Song of Solomon 8:6; Galatians 5:19)

We have the new covenant authority to BIND the spirit of Jealousy and loose the Love of God in individuals' lives!

(Numbers 5:14; Matthew 7:20; Matthew 18:18: 1 Corinthians 13; Ephesians 5:2)

Annotation #6: Standing Steadfast

Ephesians 6:10-20 - "stand" against the wiles of the devil, having done all to stand, stand. Use your weapons and stand.

Stand: (n/v)

A prolonged form of a primary old English word "standan"; to *stand* (infinitive – present form of English) transitively or intransitively as used in various applications both literally **or** figuratively as in to stand by, stand still, or stand forth; to abide; to appoint; to continue; to establish (set up) an object or state of being.

Consider the Gospel of Peace according to the connotative meaning of "peace" in the Ephesians (6:15) passage in the Word: tranquility, quietness, peace, oneness, unity, and by implication – prosperity. This is to be our attitude and posture when (standing) facing the wiles of the devil. We use our weapons, but our inward posture should be peace in knowing the battle is won by the Captain of the Host - the Lord Jesus Christ.

Annotation #7: Awareness and Strategies

Satan can and will use other persons as he attempts to bar the way to your delivery of what the Lord assigned you from eternity. Those persons will be used knowingly and sometimes unknowingly to try to cause you to have a spiritual miscarriage or to allow you to abort your dream, your assignment, your gift, your "baby".

Satan will attempt to dissuade you from gathering corporately in the House of the Lord as this is still a part of the plan since the first building of the House of the Lord at Sinai and progressively throughout the life of Israel even through The Feasts and the Feast of Booths, Tabernacles, etc.

God desires a gathering of his people and always will. However, systems of the earth have corrupted the entire idea of worship gatherings in the church; yes, the "church" as the called out ones which are a people and not a building! At the same time God ordained corporate gatherings around Him, His doctrine, Worship, and His plan for his Bride. We are His church, his Kingdom agents on earth.

We must be careful that the disappointments in some of the failures of what has occurred with and in churches does not dissuade us into thinking that we are to shift our terminology to being undifferentiated centers of learning, centers of education, community centers, etc. - being afraid to use the term "church" because of the misunderstanding of the meanings of "Kingdom" and "Church". We must pray that the Lord will raise up true, called, and set aside pastors to lead in the earth supported by the other 5-fold ministry gifts and other servant gifts given in the Scripture. There are some called to apostles, prophets, evangelists, pastors and teachers for the maturity of the saints. All pastors are not itinerate; some are called and set in the local cities as pastors of God's churches.

Thus satan, because of the power given to the chosen ecclesia, will strategically try to prohibit such powerful gatherings at Shiloh, at the church, or spiritual gatherings and celebrations established by the Lord Himself. We resist satan's false accusations and we should go to church, to Shiloh, knowing it was and is God's idea to gather.

Annotation #8: Your Song

At the initial line of Hannah's Song, she: 1) acknowledged the Lord of Hosts, 2) admitted her condition, 3) made her request, then 4) made a vow or promise to the Lord.

You can conceive a thing right where you are in the place of prayer – with just you and the Lord. You can transition that dream from a mere dream-like fantasy to a seed of <u>faith</u> that will come forth in due season.

Unharnessed, honest prayers in faith can and will produce substance! This is what Hannah's intercessory prayer did.

Annotation #9: Concluding Notes

The Lord granted Hannah's prayer request. She actually conceived during her encounter with God in the spiritual realm while in the presence of God at the Temple. Her travailing before God and speaking her complaint from her heart is what produced faith in her heart that God would answer her prayers. It also released the miracle for her to conceive when she and her husband would come together again.

Samuel's name means "asked of God", named by his mother because she had asked of God for him.

Hannah later sang a song in 1 Samuel 2:1-10 expressing her exaltation of the Lord for all he had done for her. We each have a song and many songs throughout our life time that were conceived and birthed into lyrics proclaiming the goodness of the Lord and His strength in delivering us. It is our covenant responsibility to guard our gifts and offerings, nurse/ wean them, and in the fullness of HIS time, present them back to Him as testimonies and thanksgiving for His divine victory throughout our journey to destiny! Amen.

Books Published By Drs. Michael & Cecilia Jackson

1. 9 Gifts of the Holy Spirit
2. A Synopsis: Differentiating Religion, Tradition, Church, & Kingdom
3. A Woman's Heart
4. Be Made Whole
5. Belonging
6. Beyond The Veil
7. Bold Truth
8. Breaking The Curse of Poverty
9. Get Her Back on Her Feet
10. Categorizing Spiritual Gifts
11. Dialogue Between the Watchmen and The King
12. Discern Deploy The "Heir" Force
13. Dominion For Practical Singles
14. Don't Feed The Bears
15. Finding The RIGHT Woman
16. From Press To Passion
17. Go-Forward!
18. God's Woman of Excellence For Today: The Shunammite Woman of II Kings
19. Hannah
20. It's A Wrap!
21. Kingdom Quest I
22. Make Your Valley Full of Ditches
23. Principles of the Kingdom
24. Rebuilding the Economy of the Global Kingdom of God
25. Releasing The Leader Within
26. Simply Praise
27. Step Back To Sprint Forward
28. The Bible Mesmerizing, "In-Your-Face" Info
29. TRU - The Tongue of the Learned for Cultivating Racial Unity
30. Tithing Your Tithes
31. Tool Kit for Understanding Prophets and Prophetics in the Church
32. Wailing Women Warriors Win